Village life in India

Chembakolli and its neighbours

Introduction: India – a country of contrasts 2

1 The Nilgiri Hills 4

2 The Adivasi people 8

3 Living in an Adivasi village 12

4 Farming 18

5 Local services and journeys 24

6 A living from the land 28

7 Poverty in the Nilgiri Hills 34

8 Development 38

9 The future for the Adivasi people 44

Conclusion: What is it like to live in an Indian village? 46

Index 48

CAMBRIDGE
UNIVERSITY PRESS

Introduction

India– a country of contrasts

You are going to find out what life is like in an area of southern India, around Chembakolli village.

- Write a list of all your ideas about India.
- Write down five questions you would ask to find out more about life in India.

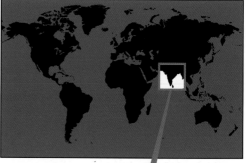

India is located in the continent of Asia. Its landscape includes many different types of scenery such as mountains, deserts, tropical beaches and plains. India is a very large country. It has a land area 13 times bigger than Britain. India has the second largest population in the world: nearly 900 million people.

This map shows the main features of India's geography. ▶

- Use the map and key to find and name:
  3 rivers, 5 cities,
  1 desert,
  5 highland areas,
  6 bordering countries,
  1 island, 1 ocean and
  1 bay.

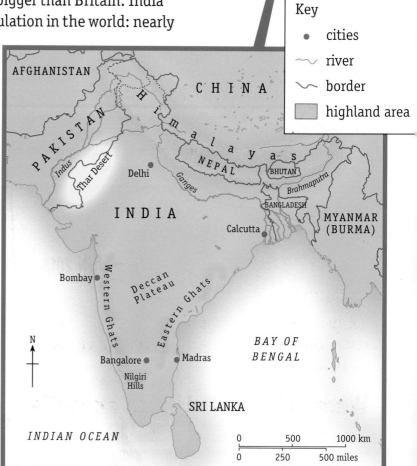

Key

- • cities
- ∿ river
- ∿ border
- ▢ highland area

There are also many different lifestyles in India. While nearly three-quarters of the Indian people live in rural areas, India's towns and cities are also very important.

▶ This is the city of Calcutta. It is home to 11 million people. Here you can buy everything you might need from a coconut to a computer!

▼ In contrast to the city of Calcutta, only about 50 families live in a village like Chembakolli.

Think about

- Compare the photographs of the city of Calcutta and Chembakolli village. What differences in lifestyle can you see?

- Which place is most like the place where you live?

You have seen some of the contrasts in India. In the rest of this book you are going to find the answer to this question:

What is it like to live in an Indian village?

The Nilgiri Hills

Because most people live in rural areas, India is sometimes described as being a country made up of 800,000 villages. Chembakolli is one of these villages. It is an area called the Nilgiri Hills.

What is the area around Chembakolli like?

The landscape around Chembakolli is very hilly. Much of it is covered by forest.

If you travelled around this area you might feel breathless walking across the steep hilly landscape. The lush green forest would reach high above you. In many places you would find large clearings where there are villages and fields. The villages are linked by dirt roads and winding paths.

The type of climate in this area is called a monsoon climate. There are three seasons: hot, cool and monsoon. Depending on the time of year, you might be breaking into a sweat as the temperature reaches over 30°C. Alternatively, you might be soaked by the heavy monsoon rains, when 30 mm of rain can fall in one day.

Think about

- How do you think the monsoon climate affects people's lives in this area?

- How does the climate compare to the climate in Britain?

◀ A sketch of the landscape around Chembakolli.

Things to do

- Copy the sketch of the landscape around Chembakolli. Add these labels to your sketch:
  forest
  fields
  hills
  house
  village
  path

The Nilgiri Hills

▼ This map shows the location of Chembakolli. It is an area called Nilgiri.

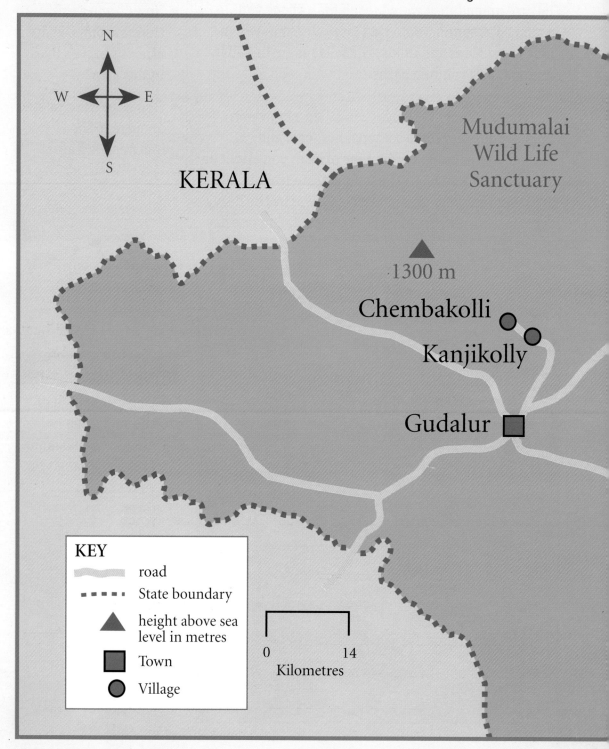

N
W — E
S

KERALA

Mudumalai
Wild Life
Sanctuary

▲
·1300 m

Chembakolli

Kanjikolly

Gudalur

KEY

~~~ road

- - - - State boundary

▲ height above sea
level in metres

■ Town

● Village

0   14
Kilometres

KARNATAKA

TAMIL NADU

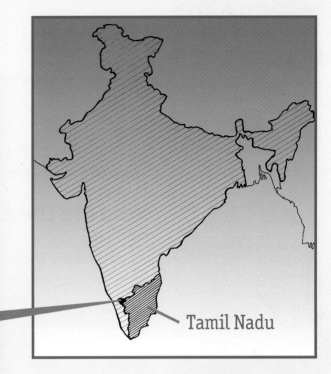

▲ This map of India shows the state of Tamil Nadu. You can also see the area of the Nilgiri Hills where Chembakolli is located.

Things to do

- What information can you find out about this area from the map? Copy out the following paragraph. Use the information on the map to fill in the gaps.

Chembakolli is located in the Nilgiri Hills. Another village in this area is_____. The Nilgiri Hills are located in the state of _____ _____. The largest town in this area is_____. Some of the Nilgiri Hills are protected as part of the_____ _____ _____ _____. This area is over_____metres above sea level.

The Adivasi people

Many groups of people live in the Nilgiri Hills. One important group is the Adivasi people. Adivasi is the name given to India's tribal people. Adivasis live all over India. There are 35,000 Adivasis living in the Nilgiri Hills.

Who are the Adivasi people?

Mandi is old but she remembers how Adivasi people used to live:

'We used to live off the forest, collecting fruits, honey and hunting animals. If we got sick we used herbs from the forest.'

Adivasi means 'the original people of the forest'. They have lived in this area of India for hundreds of years.

The Adivasis, unlike other Indian people, do not worship gods. Instead they pray to the spirits of the world around them, such as trees, the sky, plants, water, the earth and animals.

Adivasi children from the Nilgiri Hills. ▶

The Adivasi people are very poor. A typical family lives on 200 rupees (£4.00) a week. But poverty means more than just a lack of money. It also means a lack of opportunities, such as education and health care, which can allow people to improve their lives.

Things to do

- Cut out nine pieces of card. On each card write something that everyone needs to lead a good life. Arrange the cards in a diamond shape, with the most important card at the top. Compare your diamond with a partner's diamond. Discuss any differences.

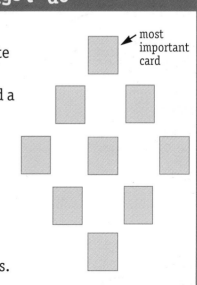

most important card

The Adivasis and the forest

The lives of the Adivasi people are linked to the forest. Because they have lived here for so long they have traditional rights allowing them to use the forest's resources. Wooden beams and thatch are used to build people's homes.

Things to do

- Use the photographs on this page and Mandi's quote on page 8 to make a list of the different ways in which the forest is used.

Wood is the main source of fuel in this area.

By clearing the forest, the Adivasis have space for their homes and crops.

Deer, rabbits, wild boar and porcupines are hunted for meat.

10

A time of change

Today the Adivasi people make their living by farming – growing crops and keeping animals. Some also earn money by working for rich farmers. In the last few years, changes have taken place which have caused serious problems for them.

In the 1980s the rights of the Adivasis to the forest were ignored by richer, more powerful people. With little money of their own, the Adivasis were unable to protect their land. As a result, some of their land was taken over by other farmers. Areas of the forest were closed off from the Adivasis. This means that the Adivasis cannot use all the forest's resources.

Mandi says:

'Now we are afraid to enter the forest, because we might be threatened by people who want our land.'

Think about

● How would the changes that have happened to the Adivasis affect their lives?

11

Living in an Adivasi village

Chembakolli and Kanjikolly are two villages in the Nilgiri Hills. About 50 families live in each village. All the people in a family live together including children, parents, and grandparents.

What is it like to live in an Adivasi family?

'My name is Chandran, I'm 30 years old. I live in Kanjikolly, just two kilometres away from Chembakolli. In my family there is Padmini, my wife, and our three children. Bintha, who is nine, is the eldest. Then there is Bomman, who is four, and Ketan, who's still just a baby. We live in a new house which was built in 1992.'

Adivasi houses have only one room. They have a sleeping area at one end and a kitchen at the other. Smoke from the fire escapes through a hole in the roof. Outside there is shade under the overhanging roof. People can sit on a bench along the wall.

Things to do

- What materials are used to build these houses? How does this compare with the way your house is built?

▲ These traditional houses are made from wooden beams, dried earth walls and a thatched roof.

▶ New houses are built to the traditional design using new materials, such as bricks and tiles.

- What are the similarities and differences between the two types of housing?
- How do they compare to the way your home is built?

13

Work

Everyone in the family has to work to make sure there is enough food to eat. Children have to spend much of their time helping their parents.

▲ Pounding rice.

▲ Picking tea.

▲ Hoeing and planting crops.

▲ Working with elephants.

Collecting water

One important job is collecting water. All the water has to be brought from the village well. It takes about an hour to walk to the well and back. Each person needs at least 4 litres of water a day for drinking, washing and cooking but only women and girls do this water-carrying job.

Things to do

Sendu is 11 years old. She lives with her mother, father and three brothers. Her family needs 24 litres of water a day. She and her mother collect this water. They can each carry 6 litres of water at a time.

- How many times does Sendu have to go to the well every day?

- How long will she spend fetching water?

- If she spends so much time carrying water, what do you think she will have less time for during the day?

A typical family day

Here is a typical timeline for a day in the life of Chandran's and Padmini's family:

Bintha is at school 20 km away. Bomman goes to the village nursery school.

Padmini cleans the house and collects water before going to work in the health centre.

Padmini gets up at 5.00 a.m. She makes breakfast – usually rice with tomatoes, chillies and onion sauce. The family eat together at 5.30 a.m.

Chandran weeds the family's field before going to another village where he runs a community group. Then he goes to work in a rich farmer's ginger fields.

- Draw some pictures of a typical day for your family. What are the differences between your day and this Indian family's day?

- Write a list of five different things about family life in India. How many similarities can you find between family life in India and in Britain?

In the afternoon, if Padmini is not busy at the health centre she works picking tea. Chandran is still working in the fields.

After school the children will have some work to do, then they can play. If his grandmother has a little spare money, she may buy Bomman some sweets.

After the evening meal, prepared by Padmini, the children go to bed. Chandran chops wood for the fire. Sometimes they go to a village meeting or a religious ceremony.

Farming

Farming is very important in India. About a third of India's wealth comes from farming. In the Nilgiri Hills farming is vital because there are not many other ways of earning a living. The seasons of the monsoon bring three different types of farming work.

How do people farm in the Nilgiri Hills?

Farming seasons in the Nilgiri Hills

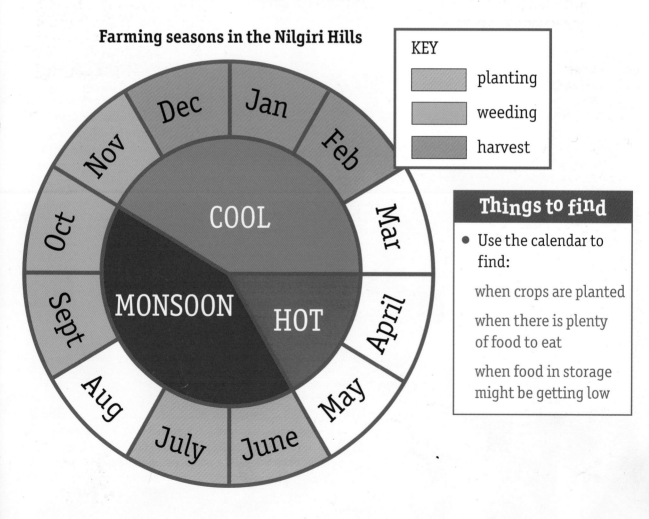

KEY

planting

weeding

harvest

Things to find

- Use the calendar to find:

  when crops are planted

  when there is plenty of food to eat

  when food in storage might be getting low

All the farmwork is done by hand. Everyone works long hours to make sure there is enough to eat. They grow bananas, tomatoes, rice, onions, peppers and other vegetables. The Adivasis also keep animals which are looked after by the women and children. Richer farmers keep a number of pigs and cows. Poorer farmers can only afford to keep one cow and maybe a goat or a few chickens.

▶ Children often cannot go to school because they are too busy helping in the fields.

▼ Elephants are used to help with forestry work such as carrying heavy logs.

Things to do

- List these jobs in the correct order. Start with ploughing.

  cooking rice

  planting rice

  ploughing the field

  harvesting rice

  weeding the field

  grinding rice

  cooking rice

Crops grown in Chembakolli

People in the Nilgiri Hills grow two types of crop: food crops are grown to be eaten by the family, cash crops are grown to sell for money. The money from cash crops is used to buy goods such as clothing and household items, for example soap, pans and batteries. It also pays for their children's school materials.

The Adivasis are too poor to grow cash crops. They grow food crops to feed their families. Their farms are very small, only 1.5 hectares (15,000 square metres) in size. To earn money they often work for rich farmers. For a day's work on a farm an Adivasi man earns 40 rupees (80p) and a woman 20 rupees (40p). Dinner is provided for the workers.

Think about

- Why do people grow cash crops?
- Can you find anything in your local shops that was grown in India?
- Why can the Adivasi farmers not grow cash crops?
- What must the Adivasi people do to earn money?

onions

potatoes

tomatoes

rice

Food crops
These are the ingredients of a typical Adivasi meal. They are all grown locally and are food crops.

okra

herbs and spices

bananas

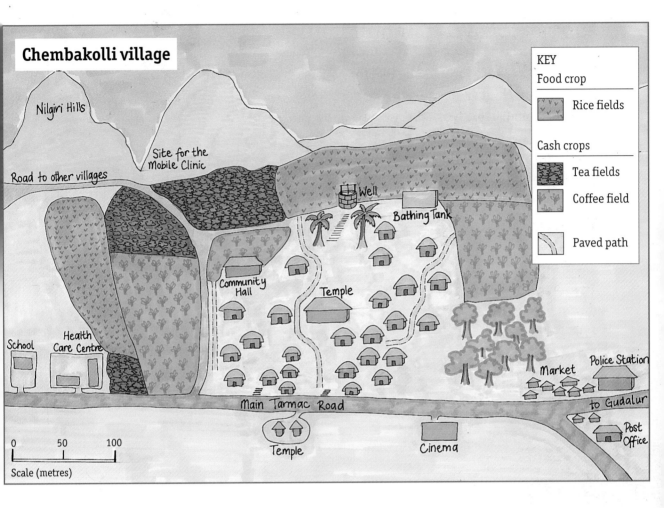

Chembakolli village

KEY

Food crop

Rice fields

Cash crops

Tea fields

Coffee field

Paved path

Nilgiri Hills

Road to other villages

Site for the Mobile Clinic

Well

Bathing Tank

Community Hall

Temple

School

Health Care Centre

Market

Police Station

Main Tarmac Road

to Gudalur

Temple

Cinema

Post Office

0   50   100
Scale (metres)

▲ This map shows the different types of crop grown around Chembakolli.
- Which are the cash crops and which are the food crops?

Cash crops

Cash crops are expensive to grow, often needing fertilisers and pesticides. Only rich farmers can afford to grow them. Ginger is a cash crop which is sent all over India. Some is even exported to Britain.

Growing ginger

A rich farmer sold his ginger crop for £2,083. This is what it cost to grow:

planting, fertilising and harvesting the ginger .... £ 312

renting a field .... £ 10

- How much did the farmer spend?
- How much profit did this cash crop make?

Tea plantations

Tea grows in large fields, called plantations. Once a tea bush is planted it must be left for two years before the leaves can be picked. The best harvests come after five years, when a good-sized bush has grown. This means there is very little profit for a long time. The bushes are picked every 15 days and a lorry comes twice a week to take the leaves to be dried.

▲ Chanda is planting a tea seedling.

▲ Women picking tea on a plantation in the Nilgiri Hills.

The Adivasi women earn money by picking tea leaves. They earn 25 rupees (50p) a day during which they collect about 20 kilos of leaves. The women collect the leaves in sacks carried on their heads.

Think about

- Why do you think the women carry the sacks on their heads?

- How much money do the women earn collecting 1kilo of tea leaves?

Recently the British charity ACTIONAID gave the Adivasis over 70,000 free tea seedlings to start a tea nursery. Now the Adivasis can earn money for themselves by growing tea.

Karunakan says:

'Tea used to be a rich farmer's crop. We knew it would be good to grow but never had money for the seedlings. Now we can also grow it.'

▲ Sorting tea seedlings at the tea nursery.

◀ 'Clipper' tea is grown in the Nilgiri Hills. It is a 'Fairtrade' crop. The farmers who grow the tea receive a fair price for it.

Think about

- Why could the Adivasi people not grow their own tea?

- How will the free seedlings help the Adivasi people?

- Why is it good to buy Fairtrade tea?

- Have you seen any Fairtrade goods in your local shops?

5

Local services and journeys

In villages such as Chembakolli and Kanjikolly there are few services such as health centres, schools, clean water supplies and electricity. However, people are able to grow most of the food they need and resources, such as water and fuelwood, can be collected from the forest.

What services are provided in the local area?

Things to do

The Adivasis earn money by working for richer non-Adivasi farmers.

- Use these pictures to make a list of how people spend their money.

Shopping

Each of these villages has its local shop, selling a range of goods. In Kanjikolly the village shop is owned by C. V. George. His shop sells bread, soap, matches, eggs, batteries for transistor radios, sweets, fruit and vegetables. C. V. George also owns a tea room. There you can buy a breakfast of tea for two rupees, and paratha (bread) with bean and masala sauce for nine rupees. The tea room is also where people find out what jobs are available on local farms.

C. V. George's Shop Price List

Soap	10p a bar
Eggs	12p for 6
Onions	11p per kilogram
Rice	9p per kilogram
Chillies	2p for 100gms

(2p = 1 rupee)

C. V. George says:

'Most days I serve 40 to 50 people. I sell 300 rupees worth of goods a day. As Kanjikolly is not a town, but a small village, my business is small. But that's how I like it.'

Things to find

- What things can you see for sale in C. V. George's shop?

▲ C. V. George's shop in Kanjikolly

Links with other places

Villages like Chembakolli and Kanjikolly are linked to other places through things such as bus services and the delivery and collection of goods.

▼ Here are some notices about what happens in Kanjikolly.

BUS TIMETABLE

9.00
11.00
1.00 } to Gudalur
5.00
7.00

TICKET 2.50 Rs

TEA
Collected twice a week

ALL YEAR ROUND

DAIRY

Collection and deliveries

8.30am

EVERY DAY

MOBILE CINEMA
NEXT SHOWING
SATURDAY

During December and January GINGER will be collected DAILY

RAVI'S
ICE CREAM

EVERY AFTERNOON

INDIA TIMES
Every afternoon

Things to find

On the notice board find five ways Kanjikolly is linked with other places.

- Which links are provided daily?

- Why does the ginger truck only visit during December and January? (Use page 18 to help you.)

- Why are there tea collections all year?

- What problems might the ice cream seller have?

Gudalur, the nearest town, has a population of over 180,000 people. It provides many services, such as large shops, cinemas and markets. This town is 14 kilometres away from Kanjikolly. However, because the roads are very narrow, winding and in a bad state of repair, it takes over an hour to travel by bus from Kanjikolly to Gudalur.

Bomman's grandmother says:

'Once a year, I take Bomman to Gudalur. It's very exciting for him to see the colourful shops, large cinemas, interesting people and auto-rickshaws weaving in and out of each other.'

▲ Towns like Gudalur are busy and crowded.

- What are the differences between the shops in Gudalur and Kanjikolly? Why are there more shops in the towns?

Things to do

Copy this table. Choose the best place for each service and complete the table. One example has been done for you.

Kanjikolly	Gudalur
small shop	supermarket

hospital   health care centre   tea room
community centre   offices   radio and TV shop

A living from the land

The land and forest are vitally important for the Adivasi's livelihood. However, other people have also moved into this area and started to use the land. Much of it is being used by government schemes, tea plantations and rich farmers. As a result there is less land for the Adivasis.

Why is land important?

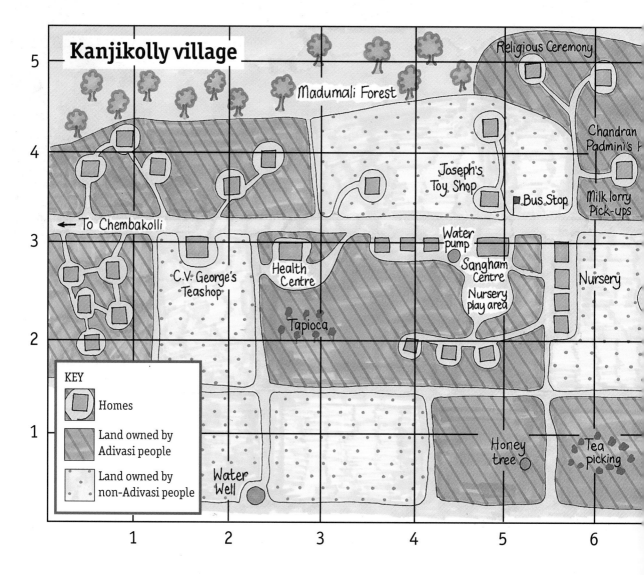

Kanjikolly village

- Madumali Forest
- Religious Ceremony
- Chandran Padmini's
- Joseph's Toy Shop
- Bus Stop
- Milk lorry Pick-ups
- ← To Chembakolli
- Water pump
- C.V. George's Teashop
- Health Centre
- Sangham Centre
- Nursery play area
- Nursery
- Tapioca
- Honey tree
- Tea picking
- Water Well

KEY

☐ Homes

▨ Land owned by Adivasi people

⬚ Land owned by non-Adivasi people

▲ Tea plantations use up large areas of land.

Things to do

- Each of the grid squares on the map represents about one quarter of a hectare (2,500 square metres). Count the number of full and half squares which are covered by Adivasi land and the number of squares covered by land owned by other people.

- How much land is owned by the Adivasis?

- How much land is owned by the non-Adivasi people?

The Adivasis are not a powerful group, and have seldom stood up for their rights. Some other people think it is easy to take land from an Adivasi person. Rights to land are written down in legal documents. But, because so few Adivasi can read and write, it is easy for other people to cheat them out of their land.

Here are two land rights documents. They are written in Tamil, a language used in this area which many Adivasi people cannot read. If someone offered you one of these land contracts to sign which one would you choose?

Think about

- If someone took something from you which you needed, how would you feel? What could you do about it?

- What do you think the Adivasi people could do to stop other people taking their land?

Contract A

எனது கிராமத்தில் உள்ள செல்வந்தக் கமக்காரர்களுக்கு தேவையேற்படும் போது இந்த நிலத்தை உபயோகிக்க விடுவேன் என உறுதிப்படுத்துகிறேன்.

Contract B

இந்த தோட்ட நிலத்தின் உரிமையாளன் நான். எனது அனுமதியின்றி ஒருவரும் இதை உபயோகிக்க முடியாது.

Things to do

- Now turn your book upside down and read in English what the contracts say.

  Contract A I promise to allow the rich farmers in my village to use my farmland when they want.

  Contract B I am the owner of this farmland. No one else can use it without my permission.

- What problem do the Adivasi face here?

- Can you find a piece of land in your local area which people want to use for different purposes?

The land ownership problems became very serious in 1988. During that year a rich farmer drove his tractor over Chorian's field. This destroyed a number of coffee plants and pepper vines. Then the rich farmer claimed the field as his own. This time the Adivasis decided to take action. Within a day over 200 Adivasis gathered on the field and forced the man to get off the land. A complaint was also made to the police. For the first time the Adivasi people had stood up to a powerful farmer. They realised they had strength when they acted together.

The Adivasi people started to map the land, showing which fields they owned. This meant that their land rights could never be so easily ignored again.

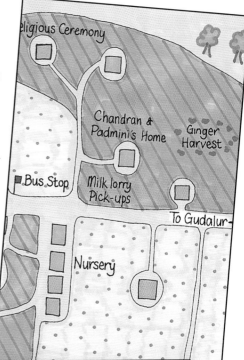

▲ Chandran mapping the local area.

Taking to the streets

While reporting people to the police started to make some immediate difference, the Adivasi people wanted to ensure they kept their land for good. The Adivasi people started to work together to protect their land. Local lawyers, who could speak both the Adivasi language and the Tamil language, were employed to check all land rights documents.

On 5 December 1988 the Adivasis, helped by a local development charity, organised a protest march in Gudalur. Because everyone thought the Adivasis were weak and disorganised the police in Gudalur only expected 30 protesters to turn up. Instead over 10,000 Adivasis marched through the town!

The demonstration worried many richer people. This is because they knew the Adivasi people had been badly treated in the past and had many complaints. They were concerned the Adivasis might want revenge and cause trouble. However, even though the procession was over 1.5km long, everything went peacefully.

The demonstration was reported in national and local newspapers. Because of this publicity the government in the Nilgiri Hills took notice of the Adivasi people's demands.

▶ The Adivasi's land rights demonstration, 5 December 1988.

Things to do

- Design a banner that the Adivasi people could have used on their demonstration to protest about land rights.

Things to do

- Imagine you were a reporter at the Gudalur demonstration. Write a two-minute radio report describing it. Include these points:

  What were people protesting about?

  Was the demonstration peaceful?

  What would you have seen?

  How many people were involved?

Poverty in the Nilgiri Hills

Although the Nilgiri Hills may look like a very attractive place, the quality of life there is very poor. Poverty is not just a lack of money. It affects many aspects of people's lives: what jobs they can get, how long they will live, how healthy they are, whether they have clean water to drink or the chance to learn to read and write. Many of these aspects of people's lives can be measured.

How does poverty affect people's lives?

▶ This diagram shows the average amount of money people have to live on for a year in Britain and in India.

India	£221
Britain	£8,320

The Adivasi people have to work hard to grow food on their farms and work long hours on other people's land to earn money. They can only get paid work during the three farming seasons. When the farm jobs have been done the rich farmers do not need any workers until the next season.

When there is no paid work it is very difficult for the Adivasi people to manage. There is no unemployment benefit in India. They manage by using any crops they may have saved, collecting food from the forest, and also by borrowing money to buy food.

Food

For Adivasi farmers, one small setback can develop into a big problem. If farmers are short of food they might borrow money to buy some. This might mean they fall into debt and have difficulties paying off their loan. They may end up cutting down on food or selling some of their land to pay off the debt.

Clean water

There is no mains electricity supply in this area and very few people have clean water to drink. Without clean water, illnesses such as typhoid can cause many deaths.

Think about

- What are the main problems faced by the Adivasi people?

- Can you think of any ways they can try to improve life for themselves?

This is a picture of the village well. The water is used for drinking as well as washing pans.

Education

Less than half the children have a school place, and even fewer actually go to school. Education is free in India but the Adivasis find it difficult to pay for their children's school materials. Many children also have to help their parents in the fields or look after younger brothers and sisters, instead of going to school.

This chart shows how many people in every hundred can read and write. 1mm = 2%
In Britain 99 people out of 100 can read.
- Out of every 100 people in India, how many cannot read? Compare this to Britain.

Britain 99%

India 43%

The average number of children in an Indian class is 41.
- Count the number of pupils in your class.

Health

This chart shows the number of people looked after by one doctor in Britain and in India.
1 figure = 100 people

- How many people are looked after by 1 doctor in Britain?
- How does this compare to India?

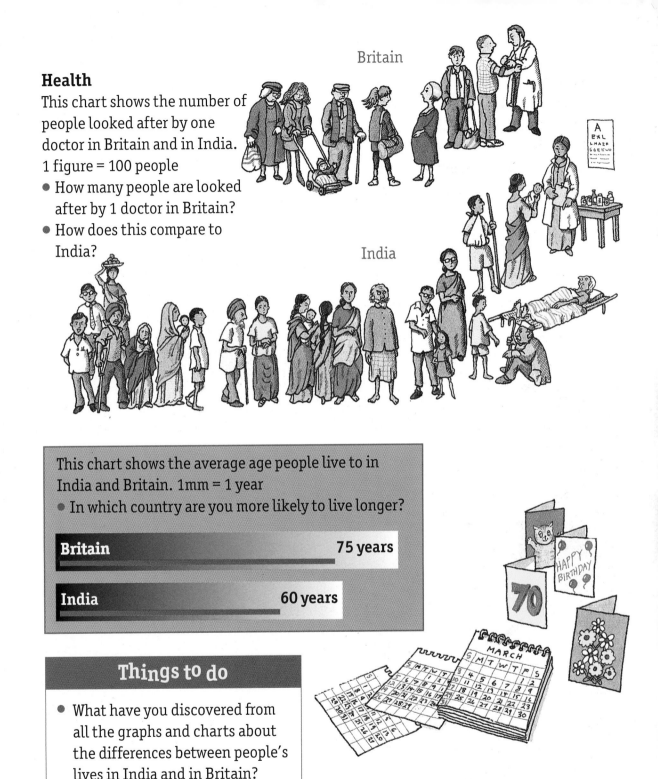

Britain

India

This chart shows the average age people live to in India and Britain. 1mm = 1 year

- In which country are you more likely to live longer?

Britain	**75 years**
India	**60 years**

Things to do

- What have you discovered from all the graphs and charts about the differences between people's lives in India and in Britain?

- What reasons can you suggest for the differences?

Development

8

When the Adivasis are asked what things they want to improve in their lives they say: land rights, clean water supplies, education, health care and farming.

How can these improvements be made?

Adivasi people meet in local community groups called sanghams where they discuss their problems and work out how they can improve their lives. Chandran, from Kanjikolly, is a local community leader. He is paid 1,050 rupees a month (£21.00) to organise sanghams in seven villages.

Because the Adivasis are poor, local banks will not lend them money. Instead they have to borrow money from local money lenders. This is very expensive. Sangham groups have started to run schemes where people can save and borrow money. The borrowed money is used to pay for food, farm tools, house-building, the legal costs of protecting their land rights and to pay off debts. Borrowers pay back this money, at low rates of interest, over a number of weeks.

▼ 100 rupees = £2.00.

Sanghams

This picture shows a women's savings and credit sangham group in Chembakolli. Each sangham brings together about 30 families. At each meeting everyone 'saves' four rupees and also an amount of rice. Everyone can then take it in turns to borrow from this fund.

Think about

- How much money will be collected at every meeting by an average-sized group?

- If you lived in Chembakolli and borrowed some money from a savings and credit group, what would be a good way to spend the money?

- How would this improve your life?

Learning for the future

Lack of education is a major problem in this area. There are few government schools and lessons are in Tamil, the state language, not the Adivasi language.

To overcome this problem, nurseries were started for Adivasi children. In these nurseries children learn about the Adivasi culture through songs and games. This gives them a good image of themselves. One in five children now attends these nurseries.

Penchi says not being taught in his own language affected his education:

'I went to a government school. The other children couldn't understand my language and the teacher told me not to speak it. For 12 years I felt everyone was superior to me.'

● What problems would you have if you had to learn everything at school in French?

▲ Children aged between 2 and 6 years old go to nursery classes like this one.

Many older Adivasi children attend secondary schools. Most of them receive extra lessons in maths, English, Tamil and science. Because there are few schools close to the villages, some children live at these schools during the week. Bintha, from Kanjikolly, boards at Kallichal school, which is 20 km away from her village.

◀ Bintha's class at Kallichal School.

Bintha's school day

08.30 a.m.	Breakfast
09.30 a.m	Assembly
10.00 a.m	Registration
	Lesson 1 – Mathematics
11.00 a.m	Lesson 2 – Tamil
11.45 a.m	Break
12.00 noon	Lesson 3 – Mathematics
1.00 p.m.	Lunch
2.00 p.m	Lesson 4 – English
2.45 p.m	Lesson 5 – Citizenship
3.30 p.m	Break
4.15 p.m	Finish school
5.30 p.m	Dinner

Things to do

- How do people's lives improve when they can read and write? Make a list of the advantages of being able to read and write.

- Compare Bintha's timetable to your school day. Make a list of any similarities and differences.

A healthy future

Many people rely on streams and springs for their drinking water. These sources are also used by animals that can pollute the water. New wells and boreholes have been dug to provide clean water.

Health centres have been set up to provide basic health treatment. Many local people volunteered to train as village health workers. In these centres babies are weighed to monitor their growth and progress. Their arms are measured to make sure they are not undernourished. If a baby's arm measures less than 13 centimetres around the fattest part they are given ragi – a special food made from millet.

13cm

Padmini is a health worker and looks after 120 families. She says:

'I tell people that many illnesses are caused by people not washing their hands after going to the toilet and before cooking. I tell them to eat healthy food, such as fresh vegetables and, when they can afford it, meat.'

To provide extra help two doctors have been employed. They train the health workers and make regular visits to the villages. At first many Adivasis were surprised to see them.

The doctors immunise children against diseases such as measles, TB and polio, and also look after the health of pregnant women. If there is a serious problem they send the patient to be treated at a hospital in Gudalur.

Dr Roopa says:

'For a year people couldn't understand why we were going into their village. Their idea of a doctor was of someone who sits in an office and just gives out pills!'

Things to do

- Design a poster which Padmini could use to educate people about the importance of health. Remember that few people in this area can read so you will have to use mainly pictures and symbols.

◀ Dr Roopa looks after the Adivasis in their village.

The future for the Adivasi people

Many of the Adivasis believe that they have made a good start. They have set up strong organisations and in future they will be able to depend on each other. Change has begun and there is no stopping it.

What will the future be like?

The sanghams have helped people to protect their land. This has greatly improved the Adivasis' lives. To celebrate the success of keeping their land, a festival is held on the anniversary of the Gudalur march. During the festival the Adivasis raise their flag and sing their song.

Chandran says:

'The problem was always land. The sangham told everyone their rights and that they shouldn't fear anyone who threatened them. So we protect the land together and our fear has gone.'

Before we came together we were in a dark place.

Now the Adivasis are coming from the dark to the light.

We became educated and now we are without fear.

Like India the Adivasis are growing strong.

Now our flag is flying.

- Write another verse to this song describing other improvements taking place in this area.

Many Adivasi parents agree with Chandran when he says:

'I am happy my family is living here because we are all working together to make life better. We hope the youngsters will have many opportunities to do well and also be proud of being Adivasis.'

Things to do

- Under the following headings make a list of the things which have helped improve the lives of the Adivasi people:
  education
  health care
  money
  land

- How do you think the lives of Adivasi children will be different from their parents?

Conclusion:

What is it like to live in an Indian village?

Think about

Do you remember the ideas you had about India before you read this book? Compare them with what you now know about life in the Nilgiri Hills.

- Which of your original ideas do you have evidence to support?
- What new information can you add to this list?
- Are there any ideas which you can prove to be false?

Things to do

Imagine you have visited the Nilgiri Hills. Using all the information you have, write an article for a colour magazine which describes what life is like in an Indian village.

To do this well you will need to include:

- a sketch map showing where this area is
- pictures showing what this area is like
- descriptions of the area and the people who live there
- interviews with people from the area talking about their lives
- changes to the environment and how they affect people
- problems and how they are being overcome
- eye-catching headlines

The Nilgiri Hills

Because most people live in rural areas, India is sometimes described as being a country made up of 800,000 villages. Chembakolli is one of these villages. It is an area called the Nilgiri Hills.

Chembakolli and Kanjikolly are two villages in the Nilgiri Hills. About 50 families live in each village. All the people in a family live together including children, parents, and grandparents.

'My name is Chandran, I'm 30 years old. I live in Kanjikolly, just two kilometres away from Chembakolli. In my family there is Padmini, my wife, and our three children. Bintha, who is nine, is the eldest. Then there is Bomman, who is four, and Ketan, who's still just a baby. We live in a new house which was built in 1992.'

Farming is very important in India. About a third of India's wealth comes from farming. In the Nilgiri Hills farming is vital because there are not many other ways of earning a living.

Index

A animals, 11, 19

C Calcutta, 3
Chembakolli, 3, 4, 7, 12, 21, 24, 26, 39
climate, 5
cities, 2, 3
crops, 10, 11, 20, 21

D doctors, 37, 43

E education, 9, 36, 45
elephants, 19

F Fairtrade, 23
farming, 18, 34
forest, 5, 8, 10, 11, 24, 28, 34

G Gudalur, 27, 32, 33, 43, 44

H health, 9, 16, 24, 27, 34, 37, 42, 43, 45
houses, 12, 13

J jobs, 14, 15, 18, 25, 34

K Kanjikolly, 12, 24, 26, 27, 28, 41

M monsoon, 5, 18

N Nilgiri Hills, 4, 7, 8, 12, 18, 20, 22, 23, 32, 34, 36

P plantations, 22, 28, 29
poor people/farmers, 9, 19
poverty, 9, 34

R rain, 5
rich people/farmers, 9, 11, 19, 20, 23, 24, 28, 31, 32
rights, 10, 11, 30, 31, 38

S sanghams, 38, 45
schools, 15, 19, 24, 37, 40, 41
shops, 25, 27

T tea, 22, 23
temperature, 5
towns, 3, 25, 27

V villages, 2, 4, 5, 21, 24, 25, 26

W water, 15, 16, 24, 34, 36, 38, 42
wells, 15, 36, 42
work, 14, 19, 20, 34